I0490813

Start Your Dream Business:
The Ultimate Step-by-Step Guide

Summary

This comprehensive guide takes you through every stage of starting a successful business. The book covers everything from choosing a business idea to launching and marketing your business. In Chapter 1, you'll learn how to come up with a strong business idea and assess its feasibility. Chapter 2 explores the importance of conducting market research and how to analyze the data. Chapter 3 provides a detailed guide on creating a business plan, including example plans to guide you. Chapter 4 covers the different sources of funding available for small businesses and the pros and cons of each option. In Chapter 5, you'll learn how to register your business with the government and obtain necessary permits and licenses. Chapter 6 covers finding a location, setting up your business operations, and hiring employees. Finally, in Chapter 7, you'll learn how to create a launch plan, market your business, and prepare for opening day.

Overall, this book is the perfect guide for anyone looking to start their own business. The step-by-step approach, practical examples, and expert advice make it easy for readers to follow along and turn their business ideas into reality.

Introduction

Chapter 1: Choosing a Business Idea
• Why having a strong business idea is important
• How to come up with business ideas
• Assessing the feasibility of business ideas

Chapter 2: Conducting Market Research
• The importance of market research in starting a business
• Types of market research and how to conduct them
• Analyzing market research data

Chapter 3: Creating a Business Plan
• The components of a strong business plan
• How to write a business plan
• Example business plan

Chapter 4: Financing Your Business
• How to determine how much funding you need
• Sources of funding for small businesses
• Pros and cons of different funding options

Chapter 5: Registering Your Business
• Choosing a business structure
• Registering your business with the government
• Getting necessary licenses and permits

Chapter 6: Setting Up Your Business
• Finding a location
• Setting up your business operations
• Hiring employees

Chapter 7: Launching Your Business
• Creating a launch plan
• Marketing and advertising your business
• Opening day preparations

Conclusion

FAQ

"Success in business requires training and discipline and hard work. But if you're not frightened by these things, the opportunities are just as great today as they ever were."
~ David Rockefeller

Introduction

Starting a business is a thrilling and potentially rewarding journey, but it can also be overwhelming and challenging. With so many decisions to make and so much to learn, it's easy to feel lost or discouraged. That's why this book is here to guide you through the process of starting a business step by step. Whether you have a clear business idea in mind or are still searching for inspiration, this book will help you define your vision, conduct market research, create a solid business plan, secure funding, register your business, set up your operations, and launch successfully. With practical advice, real-life examples, and actionable tips, this book is the ultimate guide to starting a business from scratch.

Choosing the right business idea is crucial to your success as an entrepreneur. It's important to find an idea that aligns with your passions, skills, and values, while also addressing a real need in the market. In this chapter, we will explore the process of generating business ideas and evaluating their potential. We'll discuss how to identify your strengths and weaknesses, research industry trends, analyze your target audience, and assess the feasibility of your ideas. By the end of this chapter, you'll have a clear understanding of how to choose a business idea that has the potential to thrive and bring you fulfillment.

Market research is a critical step in starting a business. It helps you identify and understand your target audience, assess the competition, and determine the demand for your products or services. In this chapter, we'll explore the different types of market research, including primary and secondary research, and the methods you can use to collect and analyze data. We'll also discuss how to interpret your findings and use them to make informed decisions about your business. By the end of this chapter, you'll have a clear understanding of how to conduct market research and use the insights gained to create a successful business strategy.

Starting a business requires careful planning and preparation, and a solid business plan is key to success. In this chapter, we'll cover the essential components of a business plan, such as the executive summary, market analysis, marketing and sales strategies, financial projections, and management team. We'll discuss how to create a business plan that is clear, concise, and persuasive, and show you examples of successful plans. By the end of this chapter, you'll have the tools and knowledge to write a comprehensive business plan that can help you secure funding, attract partners, and guide your business towards success.

Chapter 1: Choosing a Business Idea

Starting a business begins with a good idea. However, generating a viable business idea can be a daunting task. In this chapter, we'll explore how to generate business ideas and assess their feasibility. We'll cover the following topics:

• Identifying Your Strengths and Weaknesses

To generate a business idea that aligns with your skills and passions, you first need to identify your strengths and weaknesses. Consider your professional experience, education, hobbies, and interests. Determine what you're good at and what you enjoy doing.

• Researching Industry Trends

Once you have an idea of your strengths and interests, research industry trends to see if your idea aligns with the current market. Look for growing industries, emerging technologies, and consumer needs that are not currently being met.

• Analyzing Your Target Audience

To create a successful business, you need to understand your target audience. Analyze their demographics, behavior, and preferences. Determine their pain points and how your business can solve their problems.

• Assessing the Feasibility of Your Ideas

Once you have generated a list of business ideas, you need to assess their feasibility. Consider factors such as start-up costs, competition, market demand, and regulatory requirements. Determine whether your business idea is financially viable and whether you have the resources to make it a reality.

By the end of this chapter, you will have a clear understanding of how to generate and assess business ideas. You'll be equipped with the tools to select a business idea that aligns with your strengths and interests, addresses a need in the market, and has the potential to succeed.

Why having a strong business idea is important

Having a strong business idea is important because it lays the foundation for a successful business. Without a solid idea, it is challenging to attract investors, partners, and customers. A strong business idea serves as a roadmap for your business operations and growth, providing clarity and direction. It also allows you to stand out in a crowded marketplace and differentiate yourself from competitors.

Furthermore, a strong business idea increases your chances of success and longevity in the market. With a clear understanding of what your business does and who it serves, you can focus on delivering value to your customers and building a sustainable business. A strong business idea also helps you make informed decisions about your business strategy, marketing, and operations, resulting in better outcomes and greater success.

How to come up with business ideas

There are several ways to come up with business ideas, including:

- **Identify your passions, skills, and experience:** Think about what you enjoy doing and what you're good at. Consider your professional experience, education, hobbies, and interests.

- **Research industry trends and emerging technologies:** Stay up-to-date with the latest industry trends and emerging technologies that could present new business opportunities.

- **Analyze customer needs and pain points:** Identify customer needs, problems, and challenges, and explore potential solutions.

- **Brainstorm with others and gather feedback:** Collaborate with friends, colleagues, or mentors to brainstorm business ideas and gather feedback on your concepts.

- **Consider existing problems and how to solve them:** Look for gaps in the market and identify existing problems that you can solve with your business idea.

By following these approaches and being open to new ideas, you can come up with a business idea that aligns with your passions and skills and addresses a need in the market. It's important to be creative, flexible, and willing to adapt as you explore different business ideas.

Assessing the feasibility of business ideas

Assessing the feasibility of business ideas is crucial to determine whether your idea has the potential to succeed in the market. Here are some key steps to assess the feasibility of your business idea:

1. Determine the start-up costs and financial projections: Estimate the costs involved in starting and operating your business, including equipment, supplies, rent, salaries, and marketing expenses. Develop financial projections that take into account revenue, costs, and profits over the short and long term.

2. Research competition and market demand: Analyze the competitive landscape and determine whether there is sufficient demand for your product or service.

3. Identify potential customers, their needs, and how your business can meet those needs.

4. Analyze regulatory requirements and potential challenges: Research local, state, and federal regulations that apply to your business and determine how you can comply with them. Identify potential challenges, such as supply chain disruptions, economic downturns, or changes in consumer behavior.

5. Assess your resources and capabilities: Evaluate your skills, experience, and resources, and determine whether they are sufficient to launch and grow your business. Identify potential gaps and areas where you may need to seek external support, such as hiring employees or partnering with suppliers.

6. Conduct market research to gather insights and validate your idea: Conduct surveys, interviews, or focus groups to gather feedback from potential customers and stakeholders. Use this feedback to refine your business idea and develop a more detailed business plan.

By following these steps, you can assess the feasibility of your business idea and identify potential challenges and opportunities. This will help you make informed decisions about whether to pursue your business idea and how to position it for success in the market.

"The way to get started is to quit talking and begin doing."
~ Walt Disney

Chapter 2: Conducting Market Research

By conducting thorough and unbiased market research, you can gain valuable insights into your potential customers, competitors, and market trends. This will help you make informed decisions about your business, including product development, pricing, marketing, and sales strategies. By avoiding common market research pitfalls and following a structured research process, you can ensure that your research is accurate and actionable, leading to a successful business launch and growth.

The importance of market research in starting a business

Market research is an essential component of starting a business, as it allows you to gain a deeper understanding of your target customers, competitors, and market trends. By conducting market research, you can identify the needs and preferences of your potential customers, as well as any gaps in the market that your business can fill. This information can then be used to develop products and services that meet the needs of your target audience and differentiate your business from competitors.

Market research can also help you identify potential obstacles and opportunities in the market, enabling you to adjust your business strategy accordingly. For example, if you discover that your target customers are highly price-sensitive, you may need to adjust your pricing strategy to remain competitive. Additionally, market research can help you determine the most effective marketing channels to reach your target audience and refine your messaging to better resonate with them.

Overall, market research is a critical step in the business planning process and can help increase your chances of success by providing valuable insights and informing strategic decisions.

Types of market research and how to conduct them

There are two main types of market research: primary research and secondary research.

• **Primary research** involves collecting data directly from potential customers. This can be done through surveys, interviews, and focus groups. Surveys are a common method of primary research, where you can create questionnaires and distribute them to your target audience to collect data on their preferences, behaviors, and attitudes. Interviews involve speaking with individuals one-on-one to gather more detailed information about their experiences and opinions. Focus groups are another primary research method where a group of individuals is brought together to discuss a specific topic or product, and their responses are recorded and analyzed.

• **Secondary research**, on the other hand, involves analyzing existing data and information. This can include government statistics and reports, industry reports and publications, and competitor websites and marketing materials. Secondary research can be a cost-effective and efficient way to gather information on industry trends, competitive positioning, and customer preferences.

When conducting market research, it's important to choose the appropriate research methods based on your research objectives and target audience. You should also develop a research plan and timeline, and consider factors such as sample size and response rate to ensure your results are accurate and representative.

By conducting both primary and secondary research, you can gain a comprehensive understanding of your target market and make informed decisions about your business strategy.

Analyzing market research data

Once you have collected data from your market research, it's important to analyze it in order to draw meaningful insights and make informed decisions about your business.

First, it's important to clean and organize your data to ensure accuracy and consistency. This involves removing any duplicate or irrelevant data, and categorizing your data into meaningful groups.

Next, you can use statistical analysis to identify patterns and trends in your data. This can involve calculating averages, percentages, and correlations to better understand your target audience and market.

You can also use data visualization tools, such as charts and graphs, to help identify trends and patterns more easily. This can be particularly helpful when presenting your findings to stakeholders or investors.

Finally, it's important to interpret the data in the context of your business objectives and strategy. This may involve identifying areas of opportunity and potential barriers to success, and making adjustments to your business plan based on your findings.

Overall, analyzing market research data is crucial in making informed decisions about your business strategy and ensuring that you are meeting the needs of your target market.

Chapter 3: Creating a Business Plan

A business plan is a roadmap for your business, outlining your objectives, strategies, and financial projections. It is an essential tool for both new and established businesses, as it helps to ensure that everyone involved is aligned with the same goals and objectives.
Chapter 3 will cover the key elements of creating a comprehensive business plan, including:

• **Executive Summary:** A brief overview of your business plan, including your mission statement, target market, products or services, and financial projections.

• **Company Description:** A more detailed description of your business, including your business structure, legal status, and management team.

• **Market Analysis:** An analysis of your target market and competitors, including market trends and opportunities.

• **Products or Services:** A description of the products or services your business will offer, including any unique features or competitive advantages.

• **Marketing and Sales:** Your marketing strategy and plan for reaching your target audience and generating sales.

- **Operations:** Your plan for day-to-day business operations, including staffing, production, and distribution.

- **Financial Projections:** Financial forecasts for your business, including revenue projections, profit and loss statements, and cash flow projections.

By developing a comprehensive business plan, you can establish a clear direction for your business and ensure that everyone involved is working towards the same goals. It can also be a valuable tool when seeking funding from investors or applying for business loans.

The components of a strong business plan

A strong business plan should include the following components:

1. Executive Summary:
A brief overview of your business plan, including your mission statement, target market, products or services, and financial projections.

2. Company Description:
A more detailed description of your business, including your business structure, legal status, and management team.

3. Market Analysis:
An analysis of your target market and competitors, including market trends and opportunities.

4. Products or Services:
A description of the products or services your business will offer, including any unique features or competitive advantages.

5. Marketing and Sales:
Your marketing strategy and plan for reaching your target audience and generating sales.

6. Operations:
Your plan for day-to-day business operations, including staffing, production, and distribution.

7. Financial Projections:
Financial forecasts for your business, including revenue projections, profit and loss statements, and cash flow projections.

In addition to these components, a strong business plan should be well-organized, clearly written, and based on realistic assumptions and data. It should also be flexible enough to accommodate changes in the market or business environment.

A strong business plan can help you attract investors, secure funding, and guide your business strategy and decision-making.

How to write a business plan

Writing a business plan can seem like a daunting task, but breaking it down into manageable steps can make the process easier. Here are some tips for writing a business plan:

1. **Start with the executive summary:**
   This should be a concise summary of your entire business plan.

2. **Describe your company:**
   Provide a detailed description of your business, including your mission statement, legal structure, and management team.

3. **Conduct market research:**
   Analyze your target market and competitors, including market trends and opportunities.

4. **Describe your products or services:**
   Provide a detailed description of the products or services you plan to offer.

5. Develop a marketing and sales plan:
Describe your target audience and how you plan to reach them.

6. Outline your operational plan:
Explain how you plan to run your business, including staffing, production, and distribution.

7. Develop financial projections:
Create a detailed financial plan that includes revenue projections, profit and loss statements, and cash flow projections.

8. Revise and edit your plan:
Review your plan for accuracy and clarity, and make any necessary revisions.

When writing your business plan, it can be helpful to use a template or outline to ensure that you include all of the necessary components. You should also be prepared to revise and update your plan as your business evolves. A well-written business plan can help you secure funding, attract investors, and guide your business strategy and decision-making.

Business plan example

Here is an example of a business plan for a hypothetical company ABC Clothing:

• Executive Summary:
ABC Clothing Company is a startup clothing brand that specializes in affordable, high-quality, and stylish clothing for women. Our mission is to provide women with comfortable and fashionable clothing that they can feel confident in. We plan to launch our e-commerce store in the next six months and expand our product line in the following year.

• Company Description:
ABC Clothing Company is a privately owned business that is registered as a Limited Liability Company. Our management team consists of experienced professionals with a background in fashion design, e-commerce, and marketing. Our headquarters are located in New York City, and we plan to have a team of 10 employees by the end of our first year.

• Market Analysis:
The women's clothing industry is a $225 billion market in the US, with a projected annual growth rate of 3.8%. Our target market is women between the ages of 18 and 35 who are fashion-conscious and value affordability. Our primary competitors are established clothing brands, but we plan to

differentiate ourselves through our affordable pricing and unique designs.

• Products or Services:
ABC Clothing Company will offer a range of clothing items, including dresses, tops, skirts, and pants. We will use high-quality materials and offer a variety of sizes to accommodate different body types. Our clothing designs will be unique and stylish, and we will release new collections seasonally.

• Marketing and Sales:
Our marketing strategy will focus on social media advertising and influencer partnerships. We plan to collaborate with fashion bloggers and social media influencers to promote our brand and drive sales. Our e-commerce store will be our primary sales channel, but we also plan to attend fashion events and pop-up shops to reach new customers.

• Operations:
We plan to outsource our manufacturing to a factory in China to keep our production costs low. Our team will be responsible for designing new collections, managing inventory, and fulfilling orders. We will use a third-party logistics company to handle shipping and delivery.

• Financial Projections:
In our first year of operations, we project revenue of $500,000 and a net profit of $75,000. By the end of our

third year, we project revenue of $2 million and a net profit of $300,000. We plan to fund our startup costs through a combination of personal savings and a small business loan.

Overall, this business plan provides a clear and comprehensive overview of the company's mission, products, and financial projections. It also outlines a strong marketing strategy and operations plan, which are essential components of a successful business.

Chapter 4: Financing Your Business

Understanding the different types of funding options: This section will cover the various funding options available to entrepreneurs, such as self-funding, loans, grants, crowdfunding, venture capital, and angel investors. It will explain the advantages and disadvantages of each option and help entrepreneurs choose the best option for their business.

How to determine your funding needs: This section will help entrepreneurs determine how much funding they need to start and grow their business. It will cover topics such as estimating startup costs, creating a budget, forecasting revenue, and projecting expenses.

Preparing your financial statements and projections for investors: This section will explain how to create financial statements, such as a balance sheet, income statement, and cash flow statement, that accurately reflect the financial health of the business. It will also cover how to prepare financial projections that demonstrate the potential profitability of the business.

Pitching your business to potential investors or lenders: This section will provide tips and strategies for creating a compelling pitch that captures the attention of potential investors or lenders. It will cover how to create a pitch deck, craft an elevator pitch, and address common questions and objections.

Securing funding and managing cash flow: This section will provide guidance on how to secure funding and manage cash flow effectively. It will cover topics such as negotiating terms with investors or lenders, creating a repayment plan, and monitoring and forecasting cash flow to ensure the business remains financially stable.

How to determine how much funding you need

To determine how much funding you need to start and grow your business, you should consider several factors such as the cost of launching the business, ongoing expenses, and future growth plans.

Start by estimating your startup costs, which include expenses such as equipment, inventory, legal fees, marketing expenses, and office or storefront rent. Once you have estimated your startup costs, create a budget that covers your ongoing expenses such as employee salaries, rent, utilities, and marketing expenses.

It is also important to forecast your revenue and expenses for the first few years of operation to determine if you will need additional funding to sustain and grow the business. This projection should take into account factors such as market demand, competition, and anticipated growth.

When determining your funding needs, consider your business goals and objectives. If you plan to expand rapidly or launch new products, you may need more funding than if you plan to grow at a slower pace.

Once you have determined your funding needs, consider which funding options may be most appropriate for your business and start creating a plan to secure the necessary funding.

Sources of funding options for small businesses and their pros and cons

There are several sources of funding available for small businesses, including:

• **Self-funding:**
This includes using personal savings, assets, or credit to finance your business.

Pros: You retain complete control of your business and do not have to share ownership or equity with others. You also avoid the costs associated with borrowing money, such as interest rates and fees.

Cons: You may not have enough personal funds to fully finance your business, and using personal assets to fund your business can put your personal finances at risk.

• **Loans:**
Small business loans can come from banks, credit unions, and other financial institutions. These loans may be secured or unsecured, and the interest rates and repayment terms will vary depending on the lender.

Pros: Loans can provide a significant amount of funding, and interest rates and repayment terms can be negotiated with the lender. Additionally, taking out a loan can help you establish credit for your business.

Cons: Loans typically require collateral, such as personal assets or the assets of the business, and interest rates and fees can be high.

• **Grants**:
There are a variety of grants available for small businesses, particularly those that are focused on specific industries or demographics. These grants are typically offered by government agencies or non-profit organizations.

Pros: Grants do not need to be repaid and can provide a significant amount of funding for your business. Additionally, receiving a grant can help establish credibility for your business.

Cons: Grants are typically very competitive and have strict eligibility requirements. Additionally, the application process can be time-consuming and may require significant effort to secure the grant.

• **Crowdfunding:**
This is a way to raise funds from a large group of people, typically through an online platform. There are several types of crowdfunding, including donation-based, reward-based, and equity-based.

Pros: Crowdfunding allows you to raise funds from a large group of people and can be a great way to generate buzz and excitement around your business. Additionally, you do not have to give up equity in your business to receive funding.

Cons: Crowdfunding campaigns require a significant amount of effort to promote and may not be successful. Additionally, some crowdfunding platforms charge fees for their services.

• **Venture capital:**
Venture capitalists provide funding to high-growth companies in exchange for equity in the business. These investors typically look for businesses with a high potential for growth and a strong management team.

Pros: Venture capitalists can provide a significant amount of funding and can offer expertise and guidance in growing your business. Additionally, they may be willing to invest in businesses with high risk or uncertainty.

Cons: Venture capitalists typically require a significant equity stake in your business and may expect a high rate of return on their investment. Additionally, the process of securing venture capital can be time-consuming and competitive.

• Angel investors:
Similar to venture capitalists, angel investors provide funding in exchange for equity. However, angel investors are typically individuals rather than institutional investors and may be more willing to invest in early-stage businesses.

Pros: Angel investors can provide funding and expertise, and may be more willing to invest in early-stage businesses than venture capitalists. Additionally, they may be willing to invest smaller amounts of money than venture capitalists.

Cons: Like venture capitalists, angel investors typically require equity in your business and may expect a high rate of return on their investment. Additionally, finding the right angel investor can be challenging, and the process can be time-consuming.

When considering which funding option to pursue, it is important to consider the terms of the funding, including interest rates, repayment terms, and equity or ownership requirements. It is also important to determine whether the funding option aligns with your business goals and objectives.

"I'm convinced that about half of what separates the successful entrepreneurs from the non-successful ones is pure perseverance."
~ Steve Jobs

Chapter 5: Registering Your Business

Registering your business is an essential step towards establishing its legitimacy and protecting its brand. Here are some reasons why registering your business is important:

• Legitimacy:
Registering your business shows that you are serious about your business and have taken the necessary steps to establish it legally.

• Protection:
Registering your business can help protect your brand name, logo, and other intellectual property. It can also protect you from personal liability for business debts and lawsuits.

• Access to financing:
Many lenders and investors require that a business be registered before they will provide funding.

• Tax benefits:
Registering your business can make you eligible for tax benefits and deductions, such as business expenses, that are not available to unregistered businesses.

• Customer trust:
Registering your business can build trust and credibility with customers, as they know that you are a legitimate and legally recognized entity.

Choosing a business structure

Choosing the right business structure is crucial because it affects the way your business operates, your legal obligations, and your personal liability. Here are some common business structures and their characteristics:

• Sole Proprietorship:
This is the simplest and most common business structure. It is owned and operated by a single person who is personally responsible for all the business's debts and liabilities.

• Partnership:
A partnership is owned and operated by two or more people who share the profits and losses. Partners are personally responsible for the business's debts and liabilities.

• Limited Liability Company (LLC):
An LLC is a hybrid structure that provides the liability protection of a corporation and the tax benefits of a partnership. Members are not personally responsible for the LLC's debts and liabilities.

• Corporation:
A corporation is a separate legal entity that is owned by shareholders. It provides the greatest protection from personal liability but is subject to more regulations and taxes.

• Cooperative:
A cooperative is owned and operated by its members, who share in the profits and have equal say in the business's operations.

When choosing a business structure, consider factors such as personal liability, tax implications, and the level of control you want over the business. It is important to consult with a lawyer or accountant to determine the best structure for your business.

Registering your business with the government

Registering your business with the government involves obtaining the necessary permits and licenses to operate legally. Here are the steps you may need to take:

1. Choose a name:
Choose a name that is unique and not already registered by another business. Check with the appropriate government agency to see if the name is available.

2. Obtain an Employer Identification Number (EIN):
An EIN is a unique nine-digit number assigned by the Internal Revenue Service (IRS) to identify your business for tax purposes. You can obtain an EIN online or by mail.

3. **Register with the Secretary of State:**
You may need to register with the Secretary of State's office in your state to obtain a business license or permit. The requirements vary by state, so check with your state's government website.

4. Obtain necessary permits and licenses:
Depending on your industry and location, you may need to obtain specific permits and licenses to operate legally. Check with your local and state government to see what permits and licenses you need.

5. Register for taxes:
Depending on your business structure and location, you may need to register for state and local taxes. Check with your state's government website to see what taxes apply to your business.

6. Open a business bank account:
Open a separate bank account for your business to keep your personal finances separate from your business finances.

7. Obtain insurance:
Depending on your industry and location, you may need to obtain specific insurance policies to protect your business from risks and liabilities.

Registering your business with the government is an important step towards establishing your business's legitimacy and protecting your assets. It is important to check with the appropriate government agencies to ensure that you are complying with all the necessary regulations and requirements.

Obtaining necessary permits and licenses

Obtaining necessary permits and licenses is an important aspect of registering your business with the government. The permits and licenses required vary by location and industry, and failure to obtain them can result in fines, penalties, or even the closure of your business. Here are the steps you may need to take:

1. Determine the permits and licenses you need:
Check with your state and local government to determine what permits and licenses are required for your business. This may include a business license, zoning permit, health department permit, and others.

2. Complete the application process:
Once you have determined the permits and licenses you need, complete the application process for each one. This may involve submitting an application, paying a fee, and providing documentation such as proof of insurance, tax identification number, and other supporting documents.

3. Obtain the permits and licenses:
After your application has been reviewed and approved, you will receive your permits and licenses. It is important to keep these documents in a safe place and display them in your place of business as required by law.

4. Renew your permits and licenses:
Permits and licenses typically need to be renewed annually or on a regular basis. Be sure to keep track of renewal deadlines and complete the necessary steps to renew your permits and licenses in a timely manner.

Obtaining necessary permits and licenses can be a time-consuming and complex process, but it is necessary to operate your business legally and avoid potential legal issues. Be sure to research the requirements for your industry and location and follow the necessary steps to obtain and renew your permits and licenses.

Chapter 6: Setting Up Your Business

Finding a location

Choosing the right location for your business is crucial for its success. Here are some factors to consider when finding a location:

• Demographics:
Consider the demographics of the area, including age, income, education level, and cultural diversity. This information can help you determine if your target market is in the area.

• Accessibility:
Make sure the location is easily accessible by car, public transportation, and foot traffic. This will ensure that customers and employees can get to your business easily.

• Competition:
Research the competition in the area and make sure there is enough demand to support your business.

• Cost:
Consider the cost of rent or mortgage payments, utilities, and other expenses associated with the location. Make sure you can afford the costs associated with the location.

• Zoning:
Make sure the location is zoned for your type of business and that you are in compliance with local zoning regulations.

• Visibility:
Consider the visibility of the location. Is it easily visible from the street? Will signage be visible to passersby?

• Future growth potential:
Consider the future growth potential of the area. Is the area growing or stagnant? Will the area continue to attract customers and employees in the future?

By taking these factors into consideration, you can find a location that is optimal for your business and can help ensure its success.

Setting up your business operations

Once you have found a location for your business, it's time to set up your operations. Here are some steps to consider:

• Develop a business structure:
Determine the structure of your business and register it with the appropriate government agencies.

• Secure necessary permits and licenses:
Obtain any necessary permits and licenses required to operate your business legally.

• Hire employees:
If you plan on hiring employees, develop a plan for hiring, training, and managing your staff.

• Set up accounting and bookkeeping systems:
Develop a system for tracking income and expenses, paying bills, and managing your finances.

• Establish a marketing strategy:
Develop a marketing strategy to attract customers and promote your business.

• Set up your physical space:
Set up your physical space, including any equipment and technology needed for your operations.

• Develop policies and procedures:
Develop policies and procedures for your business, including policies for customer service, employee conduct, and safety.

By taking these steps, you can set up your business operations and create a strong foundation for success.

Hiring employees

Hiring employees is an important aspect of setting up your business, especially if you need help managing day-to-day operations or providing customer service. Here are some steps to consider when hiring employees:

• Determine your hiring needs:
Assess your business operations and determine how many employees you need, what roles they will fill, and what qualifications they should have.

• Develop a job description:
Develop a job description that outlines the responsibilities, qualifications, and salary for each position.

• Post job openings: Post job openings on job boards, social media, or through word-of-mouth to attract qualified candidates.

• Screen and interview candidates: Review resumes, conduct phone screens, and hold in-person interviews to assess candidates' skills, experience, and fit for your business.

• Make an offer: Once you have identified the best candidate, make an offer that includes the position, salary, start date, and any other relevant details.

• Complete necessary paperwork:
Obtain the necessary paperwork, such as tax forms and employment agreements, to legally hire your new employee.

• Train and manage employees:
Train your new employee on their job responsibilities, company policies, and any necessary skills. Develop a management plan to oversee your employees, provide feedback and support, and manage any performance issues.

By taking these steps, you can hire employees who are qualified and committed to your business's success, and create a positive work environment that supports growth and productivity.

"It's not about ideas. It's about making ideas happen."

~ Scott Belsky

Chapter 7: Launching Your Business

Launching your business can be an exciting and nerve-wracking time. Here are some key steps to consider when launching your business:

• Create a launch plan:
Develop a plan for launching your business, including a timeline, marketing strategy, and launch event if applicable.

• Build a website:
A website is essential for promoting your business and attracting customers. Consider hiring a web designer or using a website builder to create a professional-looking site.

• Develop a marketing strategy:
Develop a marketing strategy that includes advertising, social media, email campaigns, and other tactics to promote your business.

• Launch your social media accounts:
Create accounts on social media platforms that align with your target audience and marketing strategy.

• Network with other business owners:
Attend local business events and join networking groups to meet other entrepreneurs and potential customers.

• Launch your business:
Execute your launch plan, making sure to announce your business through all marketing channels, and celebrate your launch with friends, family, and supporters.

• Monitor and adjust your strategy:
Monitor your business's performance and adjust your marketing strategy as needed to reach your goals and objectives.

By taking these steps, you can successfully launch your business and build a foundation for long-term success. Remember to stay flexible and open to new opportunities, and to always put your customers first.

Creating a launch plan

Creating a launch plan is a critical step in launching your business. A launch plan outlines the key steps you need to take to promote your business and create a buzz around your brand. Here are some key elements to consider when creating a launch plan:

• Define your target audience:
Identify your target audience and understand their needs and interests. This will help you create marketing messages that resonate with them.

• Set your launch date:
Choose a launch date that gives you enough time to complete all the necessary preparations, such as building your website, developing your marketing materials, and training your team.

• Develop your marketing materials:
Create marketing materials that align with your brand identity and messaging, such as business cards, flyers, and brochures.

• Plan your launch event:
Consider hosting a launch event to generate excitement around your business. This could be a grand opening, ribbon-cutting ceremony, or other event that aligns with your brand.

• Develop a social media strategy:
Use social media to promote your launch and engage with potential customers. Consider running social media ads to target your ideal audience.

• Identify your launch partners:
Identify key partners, such as influencers or other businesses, who can help you promote your launch and reach a wider audience.

By creating a comprehensive launch plan, you can set your business up for success and generate excitement around your brand. Remember to stay organized, stay on top of your timeline, and be flexible enough to adapt your plan as needed.

Marketing and advertising your business

Marketing and advertising your business is critical for attracting and retaining customers. Here are some key strategies for promoting your business:

• Define your target audience:
Identify your ideal customer and create marketing messages that speak directly to their needs and interests.

• Develop your brand identity:
Develop a strong brand identity that reflects your values, mission, and unique selling proposition. This includes your logo, website, and other visual elements.

• Create a website:
Build a professional and user-friendly website that showcases your products or services, provides information about your business, and makes it easy for customers to contact you.

• Use social media:
Use social media platforms like Facebook, Twitter, and Instagram to connect with potential customers and promote your brand. Develop a social media strategy that

includes regular posts, engaging with followers, and running ads.

• Consider advertising:
Consider advertising your business through channels like online advertising, print advertising, and radio or TV commercials. Determine which channels are most effective for reaching your target audience and allocate your advertising budget accordingly.

• Offer promotions and discounts:
Offer promotions and discounts to attract new customers and incentivize repeat business.

By implementing these strategies, you can increase your visibility, attract new customers, and build a loyal customer base. Remember to track your marketing and advertising efforts to determine what's working and what's not, and adjust your strategy accordingly.

Opening day preparations

Opening day preparations are crucial to ensure that your business is ready to serve customers and make a positive first impression. Here are some key steps to take:

• Test your systems:
Make sure all your systems, such as your point-of-sale system, website, and phone lines, are functioning properly.

• Train your employees:
Train your employees on how to provide excellent customer service, use your systems, and handle any issues that may arise.

• Stock inventory:
Ensure that you have enough inventory to meet customer demand and that you have a system in place for restocking.

• Create a welcoming atmosphere:
Make sure your business looks clean, organized, and inviting. Decorate your space with signage, plants, or other items that reflect your brand and make customers feel welcome.

• Plan a launch event:
Consider planning a launch event or promotion to generate buzz and attract customers to your business.

• Test run:
Do a test run before opening day to identify any issues and make sure everything runs smoothly.

By taking these steps, you can ensure that your business is ready for opening day and that you provide a positive experience for your customers.

Conclusion

In this book, we covered several important topics that are essential for starting a business. We discussed the importance of having a strong business idea and how to come up with one. We also covered market research, creating a business plan, financing your business, registering your business, setting up your business operations, and launching your business.

Starting a business can be challenging, but it can also be one of the most rewarding experiences of your life. It requires hard work, dedication, and a willingness to take risks. However, if you have a strong business idea, conduct thorough market research, create a solid business plan, and obtain the necessary funding and permits, you can set yourself up for success. Remember to be adaptable and willing to pivot as necessary.

If you're considering starting your own business, now is the time to take action. Use the knowledge you've gained from this book to come up with a business idea, conduct market research, create a business plan, obtain funding and permits, and set up your business operations. Don't be afraid to seek guidance from experienced entrepreneurs or business professionals. With determination and hard work, you can turn your business idea into a reality.

NOW, YOU ARE READY!
<u>GOOD LUCK!</u>

FAQ

What is a dream business?

A dream business is a business that aligns with your personal passions, interests, and goals. It's a business that you feel passionate about and that allows you to pursue your dreams and create the lifestyle you desire.

How do I come up with a business idea for my dream business?

There are many ways to come up with a business idea for your dream business. Start by brainstorming your passions, skills, and interests. Consider what problems you could solve or what value you could offer to others. Conduct market research to identify gaps or opportunities in the market that align with your skills and interests.

How do I validate my business idea?

Validating your business idea involves assessing whether there is a market demand for your product or service. Conduct market research to understand your target audience, their needs and pain points, and the competition. You can also test your idea by creating a minimum viable product (MVP) or conducting surveys and focus groups.

How much money do I need to start a dream business?

The amount of money you need to start a dream business will depend on several factors, including the type of business, industry, and location. Create a business plan to estimate your startup costs, including equipment, inventory, marketing, and operating expenses.

How can I secure funding for my dream business?
There are several ways to secure funding for your dream business, including bootstrapping, crowdfunding, loans, and investors. Explore different funding options and consider which ones are best suited for your business needs and goals.

How do I build a brand for my dream business?
Building a brand for your dream business involves creating a unique identity and positioning that resonates with your target audience. Develop a brand strategy that includes your mission, values, voice, and visual identity. Use branding elements consistently across all channels and touchpoints to build brand recognition and loyalty.

How can I market my dream business?
Marketing your dream business involves identifying your target audience, creating a messaging strategy, and executing campaigns across multiple channels, such as social media, email, SEO, and paid advertising. Consider which channels are most effective for reaching your target audience and measure your results to optimize your campaigns.

How do I manage and grow my dream business?
Managing and growing your dream business involves developing a business plan, setting goals, and tracking your progress. Create systems and processes for managing your finances, operations, and employees. Continuously seek feedback and insights from customers and adapt your strategy as needed to meet their evolving needs and preferences.